# The First and Last Revelations of the Qur'an

Louay Fatoohi

Luna Plena Publishing Birmingham

Production Reference: 1150714

First published: July 2014

First Published by:
Luna Plena Publishing
Birmingham, UK.
www.lunaplenapub.com

ISBN 978-1-906342-18-0

The cover was designed by Mawlid Design www.mawliddesign.com.

The cover image is of the cave of Ḥirā’ where the Qur’an was first revealed to Prophet Muhammad. The author took this photo in 2006 when he went to Mecca for ʿUmra (minor pilgrimage).

# About the Author

Louay Fatoohi is a British scholar who was born in Baghdad, Iraq, in 1961. He converted from Christianity to Islam in his early twenties. He obtained a BSc in Physics from the College of Sciences, University of Baghdad, in 1984. He received a PhD in Astronomy from the Physics Department, Durham University, in 1998.

The author of several books and over forty scientific and general articles in Arabic and English, Dr Fatoohi is particularly interested in studying historical characters and events that are mentioned in the Qur'an and comparing the Qur'anic account with the Biblical narratives, other Jewish and Christian writings, and historical sources. His most recent English books are:

- Abrogation in the Qur'an and Islamic Law: A Critical Study of the Concept of "Naskh" and Its Impact.
- Jesus the Muslim Prophet: History Speaks of a Human Messiah Not a Divine Christ.
- The Mystery of the Messiah: The Messiahship of Jesus in the Qur'an, New Testament, Old Testament, and Other Sources.

- The Mystery of the Crucifixion: The Attempt to Kill Jesus in the Qur'an, the New Testament, and Historical Sources.
- The Mystery of Israel in Ancient Egypt: The Exodus in the Qur'an, the Old Testament, Archaeological Finds, and Historical Sources.
- The Mystery of the Historical Jesus: The Messiah in the Qur'an, the Bible, and Historical Sources.
- The Prophet Joseph in the Qur'an, the Bible, and History: A new detailed commentary on the Qur'anic Chapter of Joseph.
- Jihad in the Qur'an: The Truth from the Source.

Louay also publishes content on the following websites and where his contact details can be found:


- Website: www.quranicstudies.com
- Blog: www.louayfatoohi.com/
- Facebook: www.facebook.com/louay.fatoohi
- Twitter: twitter.com/louayfatoohi

# Acknowledgement

I would like to thank my wife Shetha for her careful reading of an earlier draft of the book. Shetha has always helped me significantly improve my writings through her insightful feedback and suggestions.

I would also like to thank my brother Faiz for his helpful comments.

My thanks also to my close friends Tariq Chaudhry and Ahmed El-Wakil for their useful feedback and suggestions. Ahmed has also kindly proofread the book.

# Table of Contents

Introduction .......... 9

Methodology .......... 13

The First Verse .......... 19
- Verse 96.1 .......... 20
- Verse 74.1 .......... 25
- Verse 1.1 .......... 34
- Unspecified Verse .......... 42

The First Chapter .......... 45
- Verse 2.278 .......... 50
- Verse 2.278-280 .......... 51
- Verse 2.281 .......... 52
- Verse 2.282 .......... 54
- Verse 4.93 .......... 58
- Verse 4.176 .......... 60
- Verses 9.128-129 .......... 62
- Verse 18.110 .......... 64
- Verse 3.195 .......... 56
- Verse 9.5 .......... 61

The Last Chapter .......... 67
- Chapter 5 .......... 68
- Chapter 9 .......... 70

Chapter 110 .................................................. 71

References .................................................. 77

Notes .................................................. 81

# Introduction

The Qur'an was revealed by God to Prophet Muhammad over 22 years from 610 CE when he was in Mecca until his death in 632 CE in Medina. He migrated to Medina in 622 CE. This is one verse that describes this gradual revelation of the Qur'an:

> A Qur'an which We have divided that you may read it to people at intervals. We sent it down, sending it down! (17.106)

At times an individual verse and at others a number of verses were revealed to the Prophet. As soon as a verse was inspired to the Prophet, he conveyed it to the Muslims, who memorized it, and had it written down. Leather, parchment, shoulder-bones, rib-bones, stones, and leaf stalks of date palms were used as writing material.[1] The consensus, based on Ḥadīth sources, is that the Qur'an was compiled in one volume by the Prophet's Companions after him. I find this claim extremely incredible, as it would have been in conflict with the natural course of action of the Prophet and early Muslims with regard to the Book they most revered, but this subject is outside the scope of this book.

The compiled volume of the Qur'an is known as the "muṣḥaf." This Arabic word means a "collection or volume of written sheets," but it has developed the technical meaning of the "compiled written sheets of the Qur'an."

People often use the terms "Qur'an" and "muṣḥaf" interchangeably, which is an inaccurate use. "Qur'an" is the name of the revelation whereas the term "muṣḥaf" denotes the written record of that revelation. This important distinction will be maintained in this book. The term "Qur'an" is used to refer to the revelation, whereas "muṣḥaf" denotes how this revelation is laid out in a book form.

The Qur'an consists of 114 chapters. The longest chapter, which is number 2 (*al-Baqara*), has 286 verses. The shortest chapters have 3 verses each. These are chapters 103 (*al-ʿAṣr*), 108 (*al-Kawthar*), and 110 (*al-Naṣr*). In total, there are 6,326 verses in the Qur'an.

It is agreed by all that the Qur'anic chapters are not listed in the muṣḥaf in the chronological order of their revelation. For instance, the first chapter in the muṣḥaf is not the first chapter of the Qur'an, i.e. not the first chapter that was revealed. In fact, while the muṣḥaf starts with a Meccan chapter, the next 4 chapters are all from the Medina period. Similarly, the first and last verses in the muṣḥaf do not represent the first and last verses of the Qur'an.

Scholars have disagreed on how the chapters came to be in this order in the muṣḥaf. One group thinks that it was done according to the Prophet's instructions, another believes the Companions who compiled it after the Prophet chose this particular order, whereas a third group takes the view that the order was chosen by the Prophet and his Companions.[2]

I do not think the order of the chapters is insignificant to be left to the Companions to decide or discuss with the Prophet. One modern researcher convincingly notes that if the order of the chapters was chosen by those who compiled the Qur'an and it was not instructed by the Prophet, they would have mentioned the reasoning behind the organization they chose, yet there is no such explanation. He also notes that there is no clear obvious reasoning behind the current structure.[3]

The order of the verses within each chapter is also not necessarily chronological. But unlike the case of the order of the chapters, there is consensus that the verses were ordered in their respective chapters by the Prophet. There are a number of ḥadīths in which the Prophet is said to have ordered a newly revealed verse to be inserted in a particular position in a partially revealed chapter.[4]

As the order of the chapters and verses in the muṣḥaf does not reflect the chronology of their revelation, scholars have invested considerable time and effort to determine various aspects of the chronology of the revealed text. Knowing the chronology of the revelation can be helpful, even at times necessary, for interpreting the Qur'anic text, learning about the life of the Prophet and early Muslims, and understanding the Qur'anic legal rulings.

These efforts have developed into a sub-science within the broader discipline of *ʿUlūm al-Qur'an* (The Sciences of the Qur'an). This relatively late term denotes the study of various aspects of the Qur'an and its history. One particularly famous work is *Al-Itqān fī ʿUlūm al-Qur'an* by the 9th century Hijrī scholar Jalāl al-Dīn al-Suyūṭī.

More specifically in this subdomain, scholars have been interested in identifying the first verse that was revealed on certain subjects, such as the first verse that permitted the Muslims to take arms to defend themselves against their enemies, the first revelation that dealt with the drinking of alcohol, and the first inspiration about the permitted and prohibited foods. A specific enquiry that attracted considerable interest is determining the first and last verses and chapters of the Qur'an, which is the subject of this book.

# Methodology

I would like to first explain the methodology of this study.

It is critical to note that the Qur'an does not contain a verse that describes itself or the chapter it belongs to as the first or last of the revelation. Furthermore, there is no verse whose meaning can *conclusively* indicate that it or its chapter was revealed first or last. It is possible at times to tell that a particular verse or chapter was revealed before or after another, for instance, if they can be connected to two historical events whose chorological order is known. As an example, a chapter that was revealed before the Prophet's migration to Medina is earlier than one that was revealed after the migration. However, there is no way to use the Qur'an alone to try and identify the first and last of its verses or chapters. This is why we have to rely on the Ḥadīth and other historical sources.

Additionally, there is no report in which the Prophet identifies the first or last verse or chapter that he received. The available reports convey what his wives, Companions, or their Successors have said. Some narratives about how the revelation of the Qur'an started imply that the account must have come from the Prophet. But there is no statement in which the Prophet explicitly says that a particular verse or chapter was the first or last revelation.[5]

I do not believe that the Prophet would not have recognized the last verse when it was revealed. I also find it incredible that he would not have mentioned explicitly to at least those close to him the first and last verses of the Qur'an. The inexistence of such reports looks even more puzzling given the many thousands of ḥadīth that are attributed to the Prophet covering not only important issues, but at times trivial ones. In my view, the non-preservation of this information is another indictment of the Ḥadīth literature and witness to its poor quality and unreliability. Ḥadīth narratives should be approached with considerable caution and read with critical eyes.

Muslims felt the need to identify the first and last revelations. Knowledge of this aspect of the history of the Qur'anic revelation is not only a matter of curiosity, as any fact about the Book of Allah has the potential to add to our understanding of it. The need for this knowledge is seen in the appearance of a number of different claims about the first and last verses of the Qur'an. At times the same reports also talk about the first and last chapters directly or indirectly, but there is only a small number of separate reports about chapters. It is also not uncommon for a Ḥadīth or historical source to report narratives that make contradictory claims, in some cases even attributed to the same Companion or Successor.

There is an important point that should be kept in mind. It is common practice for a narrative to use the first clause of a *verse* as a reference to the whole verse or that verse and following verses. Similarly, the first clause of the *first verse* of a chapter may be used to denote the whole of the first verse, the first and a number of following verses, or even the chapter. It is often clear from the context what the report meant, for instance, when it specifically uses the word "verse," but at times the meaning is more subtle. We will see examples of this later in the book.

Works on the Sciences of the Qur'an usually list reports on the subject of this book under headings such as "*awwal mā nazala*" and "*'ākhir mā nazala*," which mean "the first that was sent down" and the "last that was sent down," respectively. Such studies quote claims from earlier sources. The narratives are mainly about the first and last verses, with fewer accounts about chapters.

Using primary sources, I have compiled all reported claims and examined the merits of each, highlighting its strengths and weaknesses. When investigating the text of a verse for its likelihood to be the first or last of the Qur'anic revelation, I employed two approaches. **First**, I looked for any indication in the text that may weaken the claim. **Second**, I made the critical assumption that the text of the verse must be relatable to its being the very first or last of the Qur'an. In other words, I presumed that the first verse must contain something that links it to the monumental event of the commencement of the revelation, and the last verse must have something that connects it to the highly significant event of the completion of the 22-year long revelation and even possibly the imminent death of the Prophet also. As a chapter often contains a number of verses and different themes, it is more difficult to talk about the first and last chapters, unless narratives about verses can help.

On the basis of this analysis, I took a view on which claims about the first and the last verses and chapters are more likely to be historical. I say "more likely" because one cannot be completely certain that any claim in Ḥadīth or historical sources, regardless of how likely, is indeed truthful and accurate.

In drawing my conclusions, I have focused on analyzing the text of the suggested verse or chapter rather than the chain of transmission of the narrative. I have little faith in the historicity of those chains anyway. But I have still mentioned any reported weakness in the chain. I have also mentioned the views taken by scholars who examined this subject.

I have dedicated a separate chapter to each of the topics of the first verse, first chapter, last verse, and last chapter. I discussed each claim in a separate section in its respective chapter. I quoted in each section the narrative that makes the claim and any related information, before commenting on its merits.

Like any human endeavor, this work has its limitations and shortcomings. I have already highlighted some above, but unquestionably there are others that remain unknown to me. However, this is by far the most comprehensive and complete study of the subject of the first and last revelations of the Qur'an.

# 1

# The First Verse

There are four different specific claims about the identity of the first verse of the Qur'an and an ambiguous fifth. Some of these reports also talk about the first chapter. The following table lists the claimed verses and the wife or Companion of the Prophet to whom each claim has been attributed:

| Verse | Source |
|---|---|
| 96.1 | ʿĀ'isha; Abū Mūsā al-Ashʿarī |
| 74.1 | Jābir bin ʿAbd Allah |
| 1.1 | None |
| The *basmala* | Ibn ʿAbbās |
| Unspecified | ʿĀ'isha |

Ibn ʿAbbās' (d. 68)[6] report about the *basmala* confirms that it was followed by 96.1. The 96.1 claim has also been reported by a number of Successors. The claim about 1.1 is attributed to a Successor only. Three of the claims name the first verse of a chapter.

Let's discuss each in detail.

## Verse 96.1

Bukhārī (d. 256) narrates the following on the authority of ʿĀ'isha (d. 58) the wife of the Prophet:

The commencement of the revelation to the Messenger of Allah (prayer and peace be upon him) was in the form of good dreams. Every dream would come true like a day would break. Then the love of seclusion was bestowed on him. He used to go in seclusion in the cave of Ḥirā' where he used to worship continuously for many days before he longs to see his family. He used to take with him on the journey food for the stay and then come back to [his wife] Khadīja to take food for another seclusion.

This continued until the truth came to him while he was in the cave of Ḥirā'. The angel came and said to him: "Read!" The Prophet replied: "I do not know how to read."[7] The Prophet added: "The angel caught me [forcefully] and pressed me so hard that I could not bear it any more. He then released me and said: 'Read!' I replied: 'I do not know how to read.' He caught me again and pressed me a second time till I could not bear it any more. He then released me and said: 'Read!' I replied: 'I do not know how to read.' He caught me for the third time and pressed me, and then released me. He said: 'Read in the name of your Lord who has created, (96.1) created man from a clot. (96.2) Read, and your Lord is the most generous (96.3).'"

Then the Messenger of Allah (prayer and peace be

upon him) returned with it (the revelation), with his heart beating severely. He went to Khadīja bint Khuwailid and said: "Cover me! Cover me!" They covered him until his fear was over. He then told Khadīja everything that had happened and said: "I fear that something may happen to me." Khadīja replied: "Never! By Allah, Allah will never sadden you. You keep good relations with your kin, support those who have no children, help the poor, serve your guests generously, and assist those afflicted with calamity."

Khadīja then accompanied him to her cousin Waraqa bin Naufal bin Asad bin ʿAbd al-ʿUzzā. During the pre-Islamic period he had become a Christian and used to write in Hebrew. He would write from the Injīl in Hebrew as much as Allah wished him to write. He was an old man and had lost his eyesight. Khadīja said to Waraqa: "O my cousin! Listen to the story of your nephew." Waraqa asked: "O my nephew! What have you seen?" The Messenger of Allah (prayer and peace be upon him) told him what he had seen. Waraqa said: "This is the same messenger of good news (angel Gabriel) whom Allah sent to Moses. I wish I were young and could live to the time when your people expel you." The Messenger of Allah (prayer and peace be upon him) asked: "Will they expel me?" Waraqa replied: "Yes. No man came with something similar to what you have brought but was treated with hostility. If I remain alive until that day I will support you strongly." But after a short period Waraqa died. Then the revelation paused for a while.[8]

Other versions of this ḥadīth report a longer set of verses that includes verses 4 and 5 also, which make a complete unit in terms of meaning. Aḥmad[9] (d. 241) and Muslim[10] (d. 261) are among those who reported this:

> Read in the name of your Lord who has created, (96.1) created man from a clot. (96.2) Read, and your Lord is the most generous (96.3) who has taught by the pen, (96.4) taught man that which he did not know. (96.5)

There are other ḥadīths that mention these verses, but others mention only the first verse, "Read in the name of your Lord who has created," or even only the first part of it, "Read in the name of your Lord."[11] But, as I pointed out earlier, it is common practice for a report to use the first clause of a verse as an abbreviation for the whole of that verse or even including few others that follow it. Regardless of how many of these verses were first revealed, the first verse would have to be 96.1 according to these reports.

This identification of the first verse of the Qur'an is found in other sources, including Abū ʿUbaid al-Qāsim b. Sallām. (d. 224)[12] and Ṭabarī's (d. 310) exegesis[13] and history.[14] Ibn Abī Shaiba (d. 235) mentions three ḥadīths attributed to three Successors about the first revelation of the Qur'an, all of which agree that it was chapter 96 (*al-ʿAlaq*: The Clot) with two stating that it was followed by chapter 68 (*al-Qalam*: The Pen).[15]

As pointed out by Ibn Kathīr[16] (d. 774) and others, this is the claim that has earned the acceptance of the majority of scholars. Later scholars have continued to find this claim the most credible. These include classical scholars, like Suyūṭī (d. 911),[17] and recent ones, such as Ṭabaṭabā'ī,[18] Zarqānī,[19] and Qaṭṭān.[20]

There is nothing in verse 96.1, or the verses that follow it, that would suggest that it could not be the first revelation of the Qur'an. Furthermore, there are arguments in support of it.

**First**, the verse starts with the word "*iqra'* (read)" from which the name of the Book that contains the revelation — "the Qur'an" — is derived. The Qur'an acquired its name from the fact that it was read to the Prophet by Gabriel. The Prophet, in turn, read to the Muslims every revelation as soon as he heard it.

One beautiful aspect of the verse is that it makes the role of Gabriel almost completely invisible. While he is tasked with delivering the message to Muhammad, the clause "read in the name of your Lord" talks only about the source of the message, that is Allah, and its destination, i.e. Muhammad.

**Second**, it is highly likely that more than one verse were revealed first. We should expect the first revelation to have given the Prophet enough information about this monumental event and change in his life, the life of his people, and ultimately the history of the whole world. For instance, the verse "read in the name of your Lord who has created" alone would not have given the Prophet enough information. I think that the first five verses of chapter 96 where all revealed at the same time, which is what the Ḥadīth says. The reason is that they form one unit. They talk about the reading of the Qur'an, the writing of it with the reference to the pen, and the whole process of revelation being one of education and delivery of knowledge. The Prophet had every Qur'anic verse written down as soon as it was revealed.

The first verses clearly talk about the Prophet's responsibility of reading the Qur'an to people as it is being revealed to him. In other words, the verse can be understood as commanding the Prophet to be prepared to receive and convey the Qur'an. This is perfectly in line with the suggestion that it was the first verse to be revealed.

Additionally, I do not think the verses that follow 96.5 were revealed with the first five, because verse 96.6 starts a new theme. I will quote here the first ten verses of the chapter:

> Read in the name of your Lord who has created, (96.1) created man from a clot. (96.2) Read, and your Lord is the most generous (96.3) who has taught by the pen, (96.4) taught man that which he did not know (96.5). No, man indeed transgresses, (96.6) seeing himself self-sufficient. (96.7) To your Lord is the return. (96.8) Have you seen the one who forbids (96.9) a servant when he prays? (96.10)

As can be seen, verse 96.6 starts a different theme about the transgression of man. Furthermore, verses 96.9-10 clearly indicate that by the time they were revealed, the practice of praying to Allah alone had already been established and was attracting hostility. It is thought that this is a reference to the Prophet's notorious uncle Abū Jahl preventing him from praying,[21] but it could be a general reference to how the disbelievers treated the early Muslims. These verses must have been revealed quite some time after the first set of verses that announced the new religion.

I think we have a very strong case to conclude that the first revelation of the Qur'an to the Prophet consisted of verses 96.1-5.

## Verse 74.1

Ṭabarī has said that "O you shrouded in the mantle!" (74.1) was "the first thing of the Qur'an to descend on the Messenger of Allah."[22] This claim is based on a statement reported by Muslim[23] (d. 261) and others and attributed to Jābir bin ʿAbd Allah (d. 78), one of the Companions of the Prophet. According to Bukhārī's version, Yaḥyā bin Abī Kathīr asked the Successor Abū Salama bin ʿAbd al-Raḥmān about "the first that was revealed of the Qur'an," to which the latter replied: "O you shrouded in the mantle!" Yaḥyā then said that he had heard that it is rather "Read in the name of your Lord who has created." ʿAbd al-Raḥmān responded by saying that he had exactly the same exchange with Jābir and went on to quote Jābir's reply:

> I will not tell you except what the Messenger of Allah (prayer and peace be upon him) told us. He said: "I was in seclusion in the cave of Ḥirā', and after completing the time of seclusion I came down [from the cave in the mountain]. I was then called upon. I looked to my right but saw nothing. I looked to my left but saw nothing. I looked in front of me but saw nothing. I looked down but saw nothing. I then looked up and saw something. I went to Khadīja and told her: 'wrap me up and pour cold water on me.' They wrapped me up and poured cold water on me. Then 'O you shrouded in the mantle! (74.1) Arise and warn, (74.2) your Lord glorify (74.3)' were revealed."[24]

In another version of this ḥadīth, the Prophet is

reported to have said that when he looked up he "saw him sitting on a throne between the heaven and the earth."[25] The reference here is to Gabriel.

But there is a second ḥadīth attributed to Jābir that reconciles his story about how verses 74.1-2 were revealed with ʿĀ'isha's account of the revelation of the first verses of chapter 96 which we quoted in the previous section. Jābir's second ḥadīth makes it clear that the verses of chapter 74 (*al-Muddaththir*: The Shrouded One) were revealed after those of 96. This ḥadīth is reported as a separate ḥadīth and it also appears as an addendum to ʿĀ'isha's ḥadīth. Let's look at both.

The addendum is not attributed to ʿĀ'isha, but it has its own chain of transmission that goes back to Jābir. ʿĀ'isha's ḥadīth ends by saying that after Waraqa's death "the revelation paused for a while." The addendum then starts by stating that the cessation of the revelation saddened the Prophet, before going on to say that Jābir attributed to the Prophet the following words about the pause of the revelation:

> While I was walking, I heard a voice from heaven. I raised my eyes and saw the angel who came to me in Ḥirā' sitting on a chair between the heaven and the earth. I was scared of him, so I returned [to my family] and said: "Shroud me, shroud me."

Jābir goes on to say:

> They shrouded him, and Allah revealed: "O you shrouded in the mantle! (74.1) Arise and warn, (74.2) your Lord glorify, (74.3) your clothes do purify, and the abomination do abandon (74.5)." The revelation then continued after that.[26]

The ḥadīth was reported in its separate form by many, including Abū 'Ubaid[27], Muslim,[28] and Ṭabarī.[29]

The overwhelming majority of scholars have chosen to accept the reconciliation that Jābir's second ḥadīth offers. They accept 'Ā'isha's assertion that 96.1 was the first verse *ever*, and they also accommodate Jābir's claim that 74.1 was the first to be revealed *after the pause of revelation.*

But Jābir's first ḥadīth remains a problem, because it positively confirms that 74.1 was revealed before 96.1. This contradiction then had to be addressed. In his renowned classic *Asbāb al-Nuzūl*, Wāḥidī[30] (d. 468) reported that some have claimed that Jābir was not present when the Prophet started speaking about the revelation of 96.1. Having arrived late, he heard only the latter part of the Prophet's story in which he talked about the later revelation of 74.1. This explanation of how Jābir developed his *confident* misunderstanding is obviously absurd.

Suyūṭī mentions five explanatory attempts. One claims that Jābir was being asked about which chapter was first *wholly* revealed, so he said it is chapter 74, even though the first verses of chapter 96 were revealed first. In other words, the revelation of chapter 96 started before chapter 74, but the revelation of the latter was completed before the completion of any other chapter. Ibn ʿAqīla al-Makkī (d. 1150) is one scholar who accepts this explanation.[31]

The second suggests that he was talking specifically about which verses were revealed *after the pause of revelation*. The third is that he meant the first verse about *warning people* not the first verse ever. The fourth states that he referred to the first verse that was revealed *because of an earlier cause*, which was the Prophet's feeling of fear, whereas 96.1 was not preceded by a cause.

All these explanatory attempts share a sense of desperation. If any were true, we would have expected Jābir to clarify to his enquirer this distinction, but there is no mention of this in Jābir's statement.

Suyūṭī's fifth explanation, which along with the first one he finds plausible, is that Jābir was expressing his own view not quoting the Prophet, so ʿĀ'isha's ḥadīth must be considered of higher authority. Obviously, this explanation rejects the historical value of Jābir's ḥadīth.[32]

It is intriguing, however, that scholars have ignored the fact that any attempt to solve the problem of any of Jābir's two ḥadīths *must* lead to rejecting the other. If indeed he uncompromisingly stressed that 74.1 was revealed before 96.1, then it is not possible that he could have also said that 74.1 was revealed after the cessation of the revelation. At best, only one of Jābir's two ḥadīths may be attributed to him, so reconciling Jābir's second ḥadīth with ʿĀ'isha's must mean rejecting his first one anyway. This is why Suyūṭī's fifth explanation is the only credible one.

Because of the near consensus that ʿĀ'isha's account is accurate, scholars have usually accepted Jābir's second ḥadīth, which makes 74.1 the first after the pause of revelation, as the historical one of his two mutually exclusive ḥadīths. But this view cannot explain why the first ḥadīth, which conspicuously rejects the suggestion that 96.1 was revealed first, would be later made up and attributed to Jābir, if he had already agreed with ʿĀ'isha's account. On the other hand, if we presume that Jābir confirmed that 74.1 is older, then it would be reasonable to expect someone to have tried to reconcile Jābir's statement with ʿĀ'isha's ḥadīth by making up another ḥadīth in which Jābir explains that 74.1 was the first after the pause of the revelation not the first ever. There are indeed other arguments that strongly support this conclusion.

**First**, Ṭabarī has yet another version of ʿĀ'isha's ḥadīth that replaces Jābir's addendum with a completely different one. The addendum does not have a chain of transmission, implying that it is a continuation of ʿĀ'isha's story. In this version, Waraqa's words "if I remain alive until that day I will support you strongly" are not followed by reference to his death and the pause of the revelation. Instead, the ḥadīth continues to attribute to the Prophet saying the following:

> Then the first of the Qur'an that was revealed to me after "*iqra*ʾ (read)" is: "Nūn! By the pen and what they write, (69.1) you are not by your Lord's blessing mad. (69.2) You shall have a boundless reward. (69.3) You are following a great path. (69.4) You will see and they will see (69.5)." This was followed by: "O you shrouded in the mantle! (74.1) Arise and warn (74.2)," then followed by: "By the afternoon (93.1) and the night when it falls (93.2)."[33]

Incidentally, this is the closest that a ḥadīth attributed to the Prophet comes to identifying the first verse, but it does not state that explicitly. This narrative also contradicts Jābir's second ḥadīth that claims 74.1 was revealed after 96.1.

**Second**, this different ḥadīth claims that the chapter whose second verse swears by "the pen and what they write" followed the verses of chapter 96 which begins with "*iqra'* (read)." There is a logical progression here from a chapter that starts with talking about "reading" and later the "pen," to one that starts with a reference to the "pen" and "writing." The Qur'anic revelation was read to the Prophet who in turn read it to the Muslims and also had it written down.

There is another ḥadīth attributed to the Successor Mujāhid bin Jabr (d. 103) confirming that the first verses of chapter 69 (*Nūn*: The Letter Nūn) followed those of chapter 96.[34] I should note, however, that there are various claims about the chronology of the revelation of the chapters.

**Third**, there is a different ḥadīth that claims that the first verses to be revealed after the cessation of revelation were from chapter 93 (*al-Ḍuḥā*: The Afternoon) not 74. Ṭabarī attributes to the Successor ʿAbd Allah bin Shaddād (d. 82) an abbreviated version of ʿĀ'isha's account. After mentioning Waraqa's words about the Prophet, the ḥadīth goes on to say:

> Then Gabriel did not visit him (Muhammad) for a while. Khadīja said to the Prophet: "I think your Lord has forsaken you." So Allah sent down: "By the

afternoon (93.1) and the night when it falls (93.2), your Lord has not left you nor has He left forsaken you (93.3)."[35]

This ḥadīth also appears as a standalone narrative unrelated to ʿĀ'isha's ḥadīth, and Khadīja is replaced in various versions by "a woman," "the disbelievers," and "people."[36] We saw in ʿĀ'isha's ḥadīth how Khadīja believed in Muhammad and trusted that God would not harm him even though the Qur'an had just started to be revealed. She could not have been the person who later said to the Prophet that God had forsaken him.

Significantly, the beginning of chapter 93 fits perfectly with the suggestion that it followed a period of pause of the revelation. On the other hand, the first verses of chapter 74 seem to be completely unrelated to such an event.

All of this confirms that Jābir's second ḥadīth could not be historical. I believe it was authored as a response to his first ḥadīth which contradicts ʿĀ'isha's. This means that we have to choose the first verse to have been revealed to be between 96.1 according to ʿĀ'isha's ḥadīth and 74.1 in Jābir's. Of course, it is possible that Jābir's first ḥadīth is a forgery that has nothing to do with him, but this is not something we can verify.

I have already pointed out in the previous section strong arguments in favor of accepting ʿĀ'isha's report, based on the meanings of 96.1 and the verses that follow it. On the contrary, there is nothing in the text of the first verses of chapter 74 that explains why these verses would have been revealed first.

Furthermore, the creation of Jābir's second ḥadīth clearly reflects the belief that ʿĀ'isha's account was considered accurate, which in turn means that Jābir's first ḥadīth was deemed unreliable.

The suggestion of Jābir's first ḥadīth that the first verses of chapter 74 were revealed before any other Qur'anic verses must be rejected.

## Verse 1.1

Baihaqī has a different version of ʿĀ'isha's ḥadīth, which he attributes to the Successor Abū Maisara ʿAmr bin Sharḥabīl. In this narrative, the first verses of chapter 96 are replaced by the verses of chapter 1, known as "*al-Fātiḥa* (The Opening)," in addition to some other changes to the story:

> The Messenger of Allah (prayer and peace be upon him) said to Khadīja: "When I go into seclusion I hear a call. By Allah, I am afraid that this is something bad." She said: "Allah forbid! Allah would never harm you. By Allah, you keep the trust, keep good relations with your kin, and you never lie."
>
> Later Abū Bakr came in and the Messenger of

Allah was not there. Khadīja told him what Muhammad had told her. Then she said: "Go with Muhammad to Waraqa." When the Messenger of Allah came in, Abū Bakr took his hand and said to him: "Let's go to Waraqa." Muhammad asked him: "Who told you [about the story]"? He replied: "Khadīja." So they went to see him.

They told him (Waraqa), then Muhammad said: "When I go into seclusion I hear a call coming from behind: 'O Muhammad, O Muhammad!' I then run away to any place." He (Waraqa) said: "Do not run away. If this happens, stay firm until you hear what he has to say. Then come back and let me know."

When he went into seclusion, the voice called him: "O Muhammad! Say: 'In the name of Allah the Compassionate, the Merciful, (1.1) praise be to Allah, the Lord of the worlds (1.2)'" until he reached "nor of those who go astray (1.7). Say: There is no god save Allah (37.35)."

He went to Waraqa and mentioned that to him. Waraqa said to him: "Good tidings for you, good tidings for you! I bear witness that you are the one whom the Son of Mary brought the good tidings about. You are being visited by the same messenger of good news (angel Gabriel) of Moses. You are a Prophet sent as a messenger, and you will be commanded to strive after today. If I remain alive until then, I will strive with you.[37]

Other versions of this ḥadīth ignore "In the name of

Allah the Compassionate, the Merciful," which is known as the "*basmala*," to start the revelation with "praise be to Allah, the Lord of the worlds."[38] The first version treats the *basmala* as the first verse of the chapter of *Fātiḥa* whereas the second sees it as only an introductory clause to the chapter whose first verse is actually "praise be to Allah, the Lord of the worlds." There are contradictory ḥadīths that directly address the relation of the *basmala* to the *Fātiḥa*. In narratives attributed to Um Salama (d. 61) and Ibn ʿAbbās, the Prophet confirms that the *Fātiḥa* is seven verses one of them is the *basmala*.[39] Yet another ḥadīth claims that Anas bin Mālik (d. 93), the Prophet's servant in Medina, said that the Prophet, Abū Bakr, ʿUmar, and ʿUthmān all used to start the prayer with "praise be to Allah, the Lord of the worlds" and do not mention the *basmala* at the beginning or the end.[40] It is no surprise that scholars have failed to agree on one view.

So while the claim we are discussing in this section is the first verse of the first chapter in the muṣḥaf, there are two different identifications for this verse one of which is the *basmala*. I will deal with the *basmala* in more detail in the next section.

Baihaqī notes that this ḥadīth is *munqaṭiʿ*, i.e. its chain of transmission is discontinuous, which means one of its narrators is missing. He then goes on to qualify his observation by stating that if the ḥadīth had been properly preserved, then it could be a reference to the revelation of the verses of chapter 1 after the verses of chapter 96 and 74 had been revealed.[41] He had already quoted ḥadīths about both of these verses being the first, including one in which the Companion Abū Mūsā al-Ashʿarī (d. 42) states that 96.1 was the first verse.

Baihaqī's reconciliatory attempt lacks credibility. The narrative is clearly a substantially modified version of ʿĀ'isha's ḥadīth about the revelation of 96.1. It cannot be considered an independent account without rejecting ʿĀ'isha's ḥadīth.

I should also note that that Mujāhid is claimed to have said that the *Fātiḥa* was revealed in Medina.[42] This would mean that it could not have been revealed first. But this claim is uncommon. Also, the chapter looks more likely to be Meccan, as it is a short prayer that confirms aspects of the Muslim faith and does not deal with legal or other issues.

Zamakhsharī (d. 538) notes that Ibn ʿAbbās and Mujāhid have stated that chapter 96 is the first that was revealed, but he claims that most exegetes say that the *Fātiḥa* was the first followed by chapter 68.[43] This is incorrect, for as I mentioned earlier, the majority of scholars believe that the first verses of chapter 96 were the earliest revelations.

There is nothing in chapter 1, whether it starts with the *basmala* or the verse after it, that should definitely exclude the possibility of its verses being the first Qur'anic revelation. However, they are not as plausible as the first verses of 96 which talk about the subject of the revelation, i.e. the Qur'an. They do not contain any indication that this is the commencement of the revelation of the Qur'an. Furthermore, there is no credible report to support this claim.

Zarkashī[44] (d. 794) has suggested that all three previous claims that we have discussed so far can be reconciled. He states that the first verse of the Qur'an is 96.1, the earliest commandment warning people was 74.1, and the first chapter is chapter 1. He must have meant the first chapter that was revealed *in full*. But as I have already explained, the accounts about the verses of chapter 74 must be rejected and the narrative about the verses of chapter 1 is also lacking in credibility.

## The *Basmala*

The name "*basmala*" is derived from the first two Arabic words of this clause: "*Bismi Allah* (In the name of Allah)". The *basmala* is one of the most known and recited passages of the Qur'an. While it appears as verse 30 in chapter 27 (*al-Naml*: The Ants), its frequent use is due to the fact that, with the exception of chapter 9, all the chapters of the

Qur'an in the muṣḥaf are preceded by it. But, as discussed in the previous section, the introductory *basmala* is not considered part of the Qur'anic chapters, except in the case of chapter 1 where many scholars, but not all, have treated it as the first verse of the *Fātiḥa*. It does appear in the muṣḥaf as verse 1 of the *Fātiḥa*, which makes it the first verse in the muṣḥaf.

This uncertainty about the relation of the *basmala* to the chapter of *Fātiḥa* is also seen in the existence of a ḥadīth that makes the *basmala* the first verse of the Qur'an that is different from the ḥadīth that identifies it as the first verse of the *Fātiḥa*, which we studied in the previous section. Understandably, most scholars treat the *Fātiḥa* and the *basmala* as two distinct claims when discussing the different views about the first verse of the Qur'an.[45] I have followed suit.

Ṭabarī quotes the following on the authority of Ibn ʿAbbās:

> The first that Gabriel revealed to Muhammad is: "O Muhammad! Seek refuge." Say: "I seek refuge in the all-hearing, all-knowing One from the accursed Satan." Then he said: "say: 'In the name of Allah the Compassionate, the Merciful.'" Then he said: "Read in the name of your Lord who has created (96.1)."

Ṭabarī then quotes Ibn ʿAbbās as saying the following about chapter 96:

> It is the first chapter that Allah revealed to Muhammad on the tongue of Gabriel. He commanded him to seek refuge in Him rather than in His creatures.[46]

This ḥadīth makes the *basmala* the first verse that was revealed but followed immediately by chapter 96.

The only other report of the *basmala* claim comes from Wāḥidī, who attributed it to the Successors ʿIkrima and al-Ḥasan (d. 110).[47] This report does not mention that the *basmala* was followed by other verses. Wāḥidī also has a briefer version of Ibn ʿAbbās's ḥadīth.[48]

Suyūṭī points out the following about the *basmala* claim:

> I do not consider this a claim in its own right. The revelation of any chapter necessitates the revelation of the *basmala* with it.

He then goes on to state that the *basmala* "was the first verse ever to be revealed."[49] Actually, ʿĀ'isha's narrative about the revelation of the first verses of chapter 96 does not mention the *basmala*, although Abū Maisara's version does. Suyūṭī here makes an unsubstantiated assumption. The fact that almost all chapters in the muṣḥaf start with the *basmala* does not mean that it must have been sent down first or that it was revealed before every new chapter.

Obviously, there is nothing in the text of the *basmala* that suggests that it could not have been the first. But at the same time, it could not have been revealed without other verses, because the Prophet would have found it too vague and it would not have told him much about what was starting to happen to him.

Wāḥidī's ḥadīth that he attributes to ʿIkrima and al-Ḥasan may be ignored, because it is *mursal*, i.e. has a discontinuous chain of transmission.[50] This leaves the claim that the *basmala* was the first verse supported only by Ibn ʿAbbās' ḥadīth, the oldest source of which seems to be Ṭabarī. This report is of course aligned with the ḥadīth of ʿĀ'isha about the first verses of chapter 96. So it is possible that Gabriel first read the *basmala* and then verses 96.1-5 to Muhammad. However, I think the *basmala* was added to Ibn ʿAbbās' ḥadīth later after it had become the introductory verse for every chapter.

This view is further confirmed by the ḥadīth's claim that the *basmala* itself was preceded by the clause of seeking refuge from Satan, as it is a standard practice when reading the Qur'an to do that before reciting the *basmala*. In other words, Ibn

ʿAbbās' ḥadīth emulates how the Qur'an came to be read, so the likelihood is that both the seeking refuge clause and the *basmala* were not historically part of the ḥadīth. Finally, Ibn Kathīr has rejected Ibn ʿAbbās' ḥadīth as being uncommon and having weakness and discontinuity in its chain of transmission.[51]

## Unspecified Verse

There is a claim that specifies the first chapter of the Qur'an but only ambiguously. If we make the reasonable assumption that this ḥadīth implies that the first verse belonged to this chapter, then we should cover it in this chapter. I should point out that while this ḥadīth has been mentioned by Abū ʿUbaid[52] and Suyūṭī,[53] it is usually ignored by scholars because of its ambiguity. I am covering it here for completeness.

ʿĀ'isha is said to have advised an enquirer that he does not need to read the Qur'an in the chronological order of its revelation. She then went on to tell him:

> The first that was revealed of it is a chapter of the *Mufaṣṣal* in which paradise and hell are mentioned. Then when people embraced Islam, the permissible and prohibited things were revealed.[54]

Scholars have divided the Qur'anic chapters into categories one of which is called the "*Mufaṣṣal* (Separated)." These chapters may have been called so because they are shorter chapters, hence the *basmala* that separates between them appear so often. These are the chapters from 49 or 50 to the last chapter of the Qur'an, i.e. 114.

Clearly, the ḥadīth is too ambiguous to allow us to identify the chapter in question let alone the first revealed verse. Chapter 96, which we identified its first verses as the earliest ever, belongs to the category of *Mufaṣṣal*. However, it does not mention paradise and hell.

Suyūṭī tried to address the problems the above ḥadīth creates. He suggested that it may refer to one of the first revelations not the very first one. His other attempt is to say that it may refer to chapter 74, which mentions paradise and hell at the end, and that chapter 74 was revealed before the rest of chapter 96 was revealed.

If the ḥadīth is not about the first verse of the Qur'an, then obviously it does not concern us here. But if it is, then it would contradict ʿĀ'isha's other claim about verses 96.1-5, so they cannot both be accepted. In the second ḥadīth, ʿĀ'isha's refers to the first chapter in as ambiguous a way as to make identifying it impossible, hence making the information useless, which suggests to me that this narrative is a forgery.

# 2

# The First Chapter

The reports about the first chapter of the Qur'an are found in the narratives about the first verse. This overlap meant that we had to discuss references to the first chapter as we discussed the ḥadīths about the first verse in the previous chapter. But for more clarity, I will summarize briefly here the views expressed about the first chapter specifically.

The term "first chapter" is used in the Ḥadīth and by scholars in two different meanings. I will present the claims in each case separately.

**First**, the term "first chapter" has been used to mean the chapter to which the first verse ever of the Qur'an belongs. This is what one might call the standard meaning of the term. In this case, the chapter of every verse that has been claimed to be the first revelation is, by default, claimed to be the first chapter. From the narratives we studied in the previous chapter, then, we should conclude that all of the following chapters have been claimed to be the first chapter of the Qur'an:

- Chapter 96 (*al-ʿAlaq*: The Clot)
- Chapter 74 (*al-Muddaththir*: The Shrouded One)
- Chapter 1 (*al-Fātiḥa*: The Opening)
- The unidentified chapter of the *Mufaṣṣal* in which paradise and hell are mentioned

Given that the first verses of chapter 96 were the first verses of the whole Qur'an, we must conclude that this chapter was the first to be revealed.

**Second**, scholars have suggested that the term "first chapter" is at times used in the Ḥadīth to mean the first chapter that was revealed *in full*. In this case, the first verse ever does not belong to the first chapter in this sense of the term. Both chapters 74 and 1 have each been suggested to be the first chapter in this sense, to accommodate the popular view that the first verses of chapter 96 were first revealed while also accepting the ḥadīths about those two chapters.

It is a fact that at times the Prophet did not receive a chapter in full before verses from another chapter started to be revealed. There are reports, for instance, that he received verses in Medina which he added in certain parts of Meccan chapters, i.e. chapters that were mainly revealed years earlier in Mecca.[55] So the revelation of some Meccan chapters was not complete until years later in Medina. For example, the 206 verses of chapter 7 (*al-Aʿrāf*: The Aʿrāf) are all Meccan except for verses 163-170 which were revealed in Medina.[56]

We can also tell from some long chapters that were revealed in Medina that the events each chapter mentions took place over a long period of time. It is likely that verses of more than one chapter were being revealed in that time.

So while the first verses of chapter 96 represent the earliest revelation, it is possible that another chapter or more started to be revealed and were even revealed in full before chapter 96 was completed. Thus, while in the first sense of the expression "first chapter," chapter 96 was the first, it is not possible to form a firm view when the expression is used in its second sense.

# 3

# The Last Verse

There are ten different claims identifying the last verse of the Qur'an. They are listed in the table below along with the wife or Companion of the Prophet to whom each claim is attributed:

| Verse | Source |
|---|---|
| 2.278 | ʿUmar bin al-Khaṭṭāb; Ibn ʿAbbās |
| 2.278-280 | ʿUmar bin al-Khaṭṭāb |
| 2.281 | Ibn ʿAbbās |
| 2.282 | None |
| 3.195 | Um Salama |
| 4.93 | Ibn ʿAbbās |
| 4.176 | al-Barā' b. ʿĀzib |
| 9.5 | Anas bin Mālik |
| 9.128-129 | Ubayy bin Kaʿb; Ibn ʿAbbās |
| 18.110 | Muʿāwiya bin Abī Sufiān |

Interestingly, Ibn ʿAbbās is supposed to have made four different claims! The claim about 2.282 has been made by a Successor only. Another interesting observation is that verses 4.176, 9.129, and 18.110 are the last of their respective chapters in the muṣḥaf. The other claims, with the exception of 4.93 and 9.5, are about verses that are near the end of their respective chapters.

## Verse 2.278

Bukhārī attributes Ibn ʿAbbās with saying:

> The last verse that was revealed to the Prophet (prayer and peace be upon him) is the "verse of usury."[57]

Suyūṭī[58] clarifies that this is the "verse of usury":

> O you who believe! Fear Allah and abandon what remains of usury, if you are indeed believers. (2.278)

Aḥmad has a different ḥadīth which he attributes to ʿUmar bin al-Khaṭṭāb the following:

> The last that was revealed of the Qur'an is the verse of usury. The Messenger of Allah (prayer and peace be upon him) died before interpreting it, so abandon usury and all doubts [related to usury].[59]

One problem with this claim becomes clear when we consider the two verses that follow this verse:

> But if you do not do, then be aware of a war by Allah and His Messenger [against you]. Yet if you repent, then you shall have the capital of your money. You shall not wrong

> or be wronged. (279) If the debtor is in difficulties, then wait for easy circumstances. Yet if you remit the loan as charity is better for you, if you know. (2.280)

It is clear that these two verses continue the commandment of 2.278, so they must have been revealed after 2.278. This, in turn, means that 2.278 could not have been the last verse of the Qur'an.

## Verse 2.278-280

This obvious flaw in the suggestion that 2.278 was the last verse might be behind the appearance of a version of ʿUmar's ḥadīth in which he identifies the last *verses, not verse*, that the Prophet received as the "verses of usury."[60] These include verse 2.278 as well as 2.279-280. In this case, strictly speaking, the last verse is 2.280, although the three verses were revealed together. Scholars who wrote about the last verse of the Qur'an do not mention verse 2.280 as a separate claim as they do with 2.278, but this ḥadīth presents it so.

While this ḥadīth addresses the problem in the claim of 2.278, it fails to deal with another serious problem. In the early years of Islam, the Qur'anic revelation focused on introducing and expounding matters of faith and good works. After the migration of the Prophet to Medina and the growth of the Muslim community, Allah started revealing verses that established the Qur'anic legal framework. There are a few hundred verses in the Qur'an that are considered legalistic. Clarifying a legal matter does not hint directly or indirectly to the completion of the Qur'anic revelation. It does not seem reasonable to expect the last verse to be about, for example, the prohibition of usury. This verse does not give any indication about the conclusion of the revelation.

I think it is plausible that verses 2.278-280 were revealed together, as they are closely related, but they could not have been the last verses.

## Verse 2.281

According to Nasā'ī,[61] Ibn ʿAbbās said that the following verse is "the last thing that was revealed of the Qur'an":

> Fear the day when you shall be returned to Allah, then each soul shall be paid what it has earned, and they shall not be wronged. (2.281)

Ṭabarī and Ṭabaṭabā'ī[62] mention others who adopted the view that 2.281 is the last verse. Ṭabarī states that according to Ibn Juraij the Prophet died nine nights after the revelation of this verse.[63] Other reports make this period seven,[64] twenty one,[65] thirty one,[66] and eighty one[67] days. A report in

Zamakhsharī makes it as short as three hours![68]

As there is a ḥadīth that makes 2.278-280 the last verses, there is also an interesting ḥadīth that adds verse 2.281. This ḥadīth in Bukhārī mentions verses 278-281 followed by Ibn ʿAbbās' saying that "this is the last verse that was revealed to the Prophet,"[69] referring to 2.281.

There is nothing in this verse to rule it out as a candidate for the last verse of the Qur'an. But this verse is not unique. There are similar verses, like this:

> Fear the day when no soul shall pay any recompense for another soul, nor shall intercession be accepted from it, nor shall compensation be taken from it, nor shall they be helped. (2.48)

Verse 2.281 is the only one whose revelation is reported to have happened just days before the Prophet's death. Also, its mention of the Day of Resurrection maybe be seen as referring indirectly to the death of the Prophet. For instance, Ibn Ḥajar (d. 852) sees 2.281 as a likely candidate because of its "reference to the death [of the Prophet], which necessitates the completion of revelation."[70] Zarqānī also supports this claim because of what he considers its implicit reference to the conclusion of the revelation and the report about the Prophet passing away days after it.[71]

It looks to me that this would be too implicit a reference to the completion of the revelation and the Prophet's departure. However, this verse is a possible candidate.

## Verse 2.282

Abū ʿUbaid[72] says that Ibn Shihāb stated that the last verses are the "verse of usury" and the "verse of loaning." We have already discussed the former, so we will now focus on the latter:

> O you who believe! If you contract a loan for a stated term then write it down, and let a scribe faithfully write it down between you. A scribe should not refuse to write as Allah taught him, but let him write, and let he who owes the debt dictate. Let him fear Allah his Lord and not diminish anything of it. But if the debtor is of limited understanding, weak, or unable to dictate himself, then let his agent faithfully dictate. And call to witness two witnesses from amongst your men, but if they are not two men then a man and two women from those whom you deem fit as witnesses, so that if one of the two [women] errs, the other can remind her. Let the witnesses not refuse when they are summoned. Do not tire of writing it, be it small or great, with its specified term. That is more just in the sight of God, more upright for testimony, and best for avoiding doubt, unless it is a ready-money transaction between you, which you arrange between yourselves, then it is no offence by you that you do not write it down. Have witnesses when you sell one to another, and let not either the scribe or the witness come to harm, for if you do it will be an abomination in you. Fear Allah, for Allah teaches you, and Allah knows all things. (2.282)

Suyūṭī attributes Ibn Shihāb's view to the Successor Sa'īd bin al-Musayyib (d. 94), but this report talks about the verse of loaning only.[73] Suyūṭī also suggests that the four claims that we have covered so far are reconcilable:

> I do not see any contradiction between the narratives about the verse of usury, the verse "Fear the day when," and the verse of loaning. It looks like they were all sent down together in their order in the muṣḥaf, and they are all parts of one story. Each narrator has called one of these verses as the last that was revealed. That is true.[74]

Suyūṭī should have referred to the "verses" not "verse" of usury to cover verses 2.279-280 as well. Otherwise, his claim about the considered verses having been "all sent down together in their order in the muṣḥaf" would have been incorrect. More significantly, I have already shown that all the claims about verses 2.278-2.281 cannot be historical. This can also be said about the claim regarding 2.282.

The two objections to verse 2.278 being the last verse apply to the claim about verse 2.282. **First**, this verse is followed by another that clearly continues the same theme:

> If you are on a journey and you cannot find a scribe, then a pledge should be taken. But if one of you trusts another, then let him who is trusted surrender his trust, and let him fear Allah his Lord. Do not conceal the testimony, for he who conceals it, sinful is his heart. Allah knows what you do. (2.283)

This means that 2.283 must have been revealed after 2.282.

**Second**, 2.282 is a legalistic verse, so it does not have anything that links it to the completion of the Qur'anic revelation.

It should also be noted that this claim is promoted by a Successor only and does not have the backing of a Companion.

For these reasons, we can safely rule out 2.282 as the last verse of the Qur'an.

## Verse 3.195

Ibn Kathīr[75] quotes a ḥadīth mentioned by Ibn Mardawaih (d. 498) in which Um Salama, the Prophet's wife, described the following as "the last revealed verse":

> So their Lord answered them: "I do not waste the works of a worker among you, be it male or female — each one of you is as the other. Those who migrated, were expelled from their houses, were harmed in My way, fought, and were killed I shall pardon their evil deeds, and I shall enter them into gardens beneath which rivers flow. This is a

> reward from Allah, and Allah has the best of rewards." (3.195)

Suyūṭī adds more background details to this report which are likely to have come from Ibn Mardawaih's original report. He says that Um Salama told the Prophet: "I see that Allah mentions the men but He does not mention the women," so the following was revealed:

> Do not covet that with which Allah has preferred some of you over the others. The men shall have a portion of what they earn, and the women a portion of what they earn. Ask Allah for His favor. Allah knows everything. (4.32)

Then the following verse was revealed:

> The Muslim men and the Muslim women, the believing men and the believing women, the obedient men and the obedient women, the truthful men and the truthful women, the patient men and the patient women, the humble men and the humble women, the men and the women who give in charity, the men who fast and the women who fast, the men and the women who guard their private parts, the men and the women who remember Allah much — for them Allah has prepared forgiveness and a mighty wage. (33.35)

Suyūṭī goes on to say "then this verse (3.195) was sent down, so it was the last of the three [verses] to be revealed, or the last of the revelation before which the inspiration was specifically about the men."[76] The second possibility does not seem to make sense because, given the story, it would mean that these are the only verses that talk about both men and women, which is wrong.

Obviously, the first possibility that Suyūṭī mentions means that 3.195 was not claimed to be the last verse ever. Significantly, Ṭabarī's version of this ḥadīth also does not make this claim. Um Salama is reported to have told the Prophet: "I have not heard Allah mention women after the migration," meaning that the Qur'anic revelation in Medina had said nothing about women. The ḥadīth goes on to state that after this verse 3.195 was revealed. Crucially, it does not make the claim that this is "the last revealed verse."[77]

I should also note that the story itself is rather absurd.

Verse 3.195 is one of many verses in which Allah describes good works and confirms His reward for the good-doers. Additionally, it does not contain the slightest hint to the conclusion of the revelation of the Qur'an. I do not believe 3.195 was the last Qur'anic verse that Allah revealed to the Prophet.

## Verse 4.93

Bukhārī reported that Ibn ʿAbbās said that the following verse is "the last that was revealed, and it was not abrogated by anything":[78]

> He who intentionally kills a believer his recompense will be hell in which he shall dwell forever, Allah shall have wrath on him, will curse him, and will have for him a grave torment. (4.93)

According to Nasā'ī, Ibn ʿAbbās was not specific that it was the last verse, reporting his statement as follows instead:

> It was revealed among the last that was revealed, and it was not abrogated by anything."[79]

This verse does not show any relation to the completion of the Qur'anic revelation, so it is unlikely to have been the last verse. Furthermore, the reference to it not being the subject of abrogation might explain why a claim has appeared about its being the last revelation of the Qur'an.

I have discussed abrogation in detail in my book *Abrogation in the Qur'an and Islamic Law*, but it suffices here to say that it is a complicated and confused legal principle that has acquired a number of different and conflicting meanings. Its most common definition is "the annulment of a divine ruling by a later divine ruling." A divine ruling maybe a Qur'anic verse or a Prophetic saying or action.

So clearly the ḥadīth above is trying to stress that Allah's ruling in 4.93 regarding the intentional killing of a believer has not been abrogated. To make the case even stronger, a claim was added describing this verse as the last or among the last revelation, because this would mean the ruling is still valid.

So I do not think that 4.93 is the last verse of the Qur'an.

## Verse 4.176

Bukhārī[80] attributed the Companion al-Barā' b. ʿĀzib (d. 72) as saying that "the last verse that was revealed is this":

> They will ask you [O Muhammad!] for a ruling. Say: "Allah rules for you concerning the remote kinship. If a man dies having no children, but he has a sister, she shall have half of what he leaves, and he is her heir if she has no children. If there are two sisters, they shall receive two-thirds of what he leaves. If there are men and women siblings, the male shall get the share of two females. Allah explains to you lest you go astray. Allah knows all things. (4.176)

Suyūṭī has tried to reconcile this claim with others by suggesting that al-Barā' meant to say that this is the last verse about obligatory duties.[81]

This is another case of a legalistic verse, this time on a particular case of inheritance. Also, it provides no indication of a conclusion to the revelation of the Qur'an. Verse 4.176 could not have been the last verse of the Qur'an.

## Verse 9.5

Ibn Māja[82] (d. 273) states that Anas bin Mālik described the following verse as "the last of what Allah sent down":

> When the Inviolable Months have passed away, kill the polytheists wherever you find them. Seize them, besiege them, and wait for them at every place of observation. If they repent, observe prayer, and pay the obligatory alms then let them go their way. Allah is forgiving, merciful. (9.5)

Some scholars have claimed that this verse has abrogated numerous verses that call on the Muslims to be tolerant, forgiving, and patient, and to display such positive attributes toward non-Muslims that allowed Muslims to live peacefully with various religious groups for fourteen centuries. It has been, therefore, called "the verse of the sword." I have discussed elsewhere in detail the false abrogation claims about this verse.[83]

Like many other verses that instruct the Muslims about how to deal with their enemies, this verse has no link to the completion of the Qur'anic revelation. The claim that it is the last verse is a blatant attempt to stress that it was later than the numerous verses that command the Muslims to live peacefully with those who do not show hostility to them, even if they followed different faiths, so it can be claimed that 9.5 abrogated all those verses.

In the same way that 9.5 did not abrogate any of those verses, it is not the last verse of the Qur'an.

## Verses 9.128-129

Ṭabarī has reported on the authority of Ibn ʿAbbās that the Companion Ubayy bin Kaʿb described the following as "the last revealed verse of the Qur'an":

> There has come to you a Messenger from among yourselves, grievous to him is your suffering, careful over you, compassionate and merciful for the believers. (9.128)

In another ḥadīth that is also attributed to Ubayy, once through the Successor Qatāda bin Diʿāma al-Sadūsī (d. 117) and another via Yūsuf bin Mahrān, he is reported to have said that the most recent of the Qur'an are the following two verses:

> There has come to you a Messenger from among yourselves, grievous to him is your suffering, careful over you, compassionate and merciful for the believers. (9.128) If they turn away, say "Allah suffices me. There is no god but He. In Him I trust. He is the Lord of the great throne." (9.129)[84]

It looks highly likely that these two verses were revealed at the same time, as verse 9.129 continues Allah's statement in 9.128. Accordingly, 9.128

could not have been the last verse, so we are left with the report that 9.128 and 9.129 were revealed last, making 9.129 the last verse.

The change of the addressee in the two verses is fascinating. The first verse addresses people in general, confirming that Muhammad was sent to them as a Messenger. The second verse addresses Muhammad, giving him support to continue his mission. It is like Allah spoke to people about the Prophet, but they turned away from him, so in turn Allah turned away from them.

Verses 9.128-129 feature in a ḥadīth about the compilation of the Qur'an. After the battle of Yamāma in year 11, Zaid bin Thābit started compiling the Qur'an at the instruction of Abū Bakr. Having consulted written records of the Qur'an and memorizers of the Qur'an, he found verses 9.128-129 in the possession of one person only, the Companion Khuzaima al-Anṣārī (d. 37).[85] This story may suggest that these verses were not widely recorded and memorized because they were the last revelation. But there are several reasons for dismissing this claim; I will mention two of them. **First**, the compilation of the Qur'an started many months after the death of the Prophet, so even if these verses were revealed shortly before his departure, there would have been enough time for the verses to become known to all. **Second**, the claim that any verse was unknown to any of the Prophet's closer Companions is incredible. As I mentioned earlier, the idea that the Qur'an was not compiled during the life of the Prophet is utterly unconvincing. So this report does not represent evidence that verses 9.128-129 are the last verses.

Verse 9.129 instructs the Prophet about how he should react to those who have rejected his message. This suggests that the verse was revealed when there was still a long struggle ahead of him as he continues proclaiming his message to people.

Also, the theme of verse 9.129 is not unique as there are several similar verses that talk about people's rejection of the Prophet's message and his continued struggle in the face of this resistance, such as the following Meccan verse:

> But if they turn away say: "I have proclaimed to you all equally, even though I do not know how near or far what you are promised." (21.109)

For these reasons, verse 9.129, like 9.128, could not be the last verse of the Qur'an.

## Verse 18.110

Muʿāwiya bin Abī Sufiān (d. 60) was heard reciting on the pulpit the verse: "Let him who hopes to meet his Lord do good works and refrain from associating anyone in worshiping his Lord." He then said: "It is the last verse that was sent down of the Qur'an."[86] This is the full text of the verse:

> Say [O Muhammad!]: "I am only a human like you. It is being revealed to me that your Lord is one. Let him who hopes to meet his Lord do good works and refrain from associating anyone in worshiping his Lord." (18.110)

Here also we have a verse that does not have anything that links it to the completion of the Qur'anic revelation. Even more crucial is that the words "*it is being revealed to me*" clearly describe an ongoing process of revelation at the time, so this verse could not have been revealed even close to the conclusion of the Qur'an. Furthermore, like the argument we made about the case of verse 3.195, there are many similar verses that confirm various aspects of the creeds of Islam, so it is highly unlikely that any of these, including 18.110, is the last verse of the Qur'an.

# 4

# The Last Chapter

There are three claims in this category, as shown in the table below:

| Verse | Source |
|---|---|
| Chapter 5 (*al-Mā'ida*: The Table) | 'Ā'isha; 'Abd Allah bin 'Amarū |
| Chapter 9 (*al-Tawba*: The Repentance) | Al-Barā' b. 'Āzib |
| Chapter 110 (*al-Fatḥ*: The Conquest) | Ibn 'Abbās |

The available narratives and scholars distinguish between the last chapter that was sent down, the last chapter that was *completed*, and the last chapter that was sent down *as a whole*. The latter clearly denotes the last chapter whose verses were all revealed at the same time. The other two, however, remain ambiguous, not least because there are not linked to the revelation of the verse of the Qur'an. Differentiating between these two without any overlap or contradiction leads to the following definitions:

- The last chapter: The one whose revelation started last. In other words, it is the chapter whose first verse was revealed after at least one verse had been revealed from each of the other 113 chapters.
- The last chapter that was completed: The last chapter to have all its verses revealed over a period of time during which no verses from other chapters were revealed.

Unlike the unambiguous term "the last verse," the description of "the last chapter" is not that clear, forcing one to make assumptions as to what the different versions of this expression exactly mean. Adding to that the fact that a chapter might have had verses revealed at different times, the best one can tell is how late certain parts of a chapter might be. We can talk or how late a chapter is only in this sense.

There are three chapters each of which has been described using one or more of those three classifications.

## Chapter 5 (*Al-Mā'ida*: The Table)

This has been described as the last chapter by the

Companion ʿAbd Allah bin ʿAmr (d. 63), as reported by Tirmidhī[87] and Baihaqī.[88] Baihaqī and Nasāʾī[89] also attribute this claim to ʿĀʾisha. She told someone the following about chapter 5:

> It is the last chapter that was sent down. Whatever is permissible in it, treat it as permissible, and whatever is prohibited in it, treat as prohibited.[90]

ʿĀʾisha means that as this chapter was revealed last, none of its rulings were changed or abrogated later, so the Muslims should consider all of those rulings valid.

This chapter contains the following passage:

> Today I have perfected your religion for you, I have completed My blessing on you, and I have approved Islam for your religion. (5.3)

This passage of verse 5.3 is popularly believed by lay Muslims to be the last verse of the Qur'an, but this belief is not based on any documentary evidence. It is not clear how this belief developed and spread this wide, but it may have something to do with the wording of the verse that clearly suggests that that it is very late, which is something the ḥadīth also confirms.

ʿUmar has said that this passage was revealed on a Friday when the Prophet was on the mountain of

ʿArafa.[91] Other narratives further specify that this was during the Prophet's last pilgrimage, which is said to have taken place shortly before his death, which some sources specify as eighty one days.[92] The passage does look quite late. This suggests that chapter 5 contains one of the last verses, but that still does not necessary mean it is the last chapter, in whichever sense of this description.

## Chapter 9 (*Al-Tawba*: The Repentance)

Al-Barāʾ is reported by Bukhārī,[93] Nasāʾī,[94] and others to have said that this was the last chapter. But other versions of the ḥadīth have him describing it as "the last chapter that was revealed *complete*." The word "complete" translates the Arabic word "*tāmma*" in the versions of Ibn Abī Shaiba,[95] Bukhārī,[96] and Muslim, and "*kāmila*" in another version in Muslim.[97]

Since some versions of al-Barāʾs ḥadīth mention also that the last verse is 4.176, the ḥadīth could not have meant that chapter 9 was the last chapter to be completed by the revelation of the very last verse. This is why I suggested the meaning discussed earlier for the concept of being revealed *complete*. But looking at the text of the chapter, it is difficult to confirm that this is how the chapter was revealed.

Historical sources suggest that the first verses of

this chapter were revealed in the last month of the year 9 after the migration of the Prophet to Medina, i.e. one year before verse 5.3 above.[98] It is also clear from this and the nature of other verses in the chapter that this is one of the last chapters of the Qur'an. Indeed, ʿUthmān bin ʿAffān (d. 35) described this chapter as being "among the last of the Qur'an,"[99] which means it was not the last chapter.

## Chapter 110 (*Al-Fatḥ*: The Conquest)

According to Nasā'ī,[100] Ibn ʿAbbās tested someone whether he knew "the last chapter that was revealed of the Qur'an." The person replied that it is the chapter of "when the help of Allah comes and the conquest," which Ibn ʿAbbās confirmed. The three verses of this chapter, which is one of the three shortest chapters of the Qur'an, are tightly linked to each other so they must have been revealed together. This is the full text of the chapter:

> When the help of Allah comes and the conquest, (110.1) and you see people entering into the religion of Allah in crowds, (110.2) then glorify your Lord with praise and seek His forgiveness. He is forgiving. (110.3)

Indeed, another version of the ḥadīth reported in Muslim,[101] Ibn Abī Shaiba,[102] and others modifies

Ibn ʿAbbās' question to be about the last chapter that was revealed *as a whole* (*jamīʿan*).

As for how late this chapter might be, there is a ḥadīth that provides us with contradictory information. According to Ibn ʿAbbās, this chapter referred to the death of the Prophet and indicated that its sign is the conquest of Mecca by the Muslims, which is how he interpreted "the conquest."[103] These two claims are irreconcilable, because the Prophet conquered Mecca in Ramadan of year 8, that is about two and a half years before his death. There is another interpretation of "the conquest" as being about "conquering cities and palaces"[104] which avoids this conflict.

Taking a view on how late this chapter is depends on how one understands the term "the conquest." If it is indeed a reference to the Muslims' victorious entry of Mecca, then it cannot be considered late, but if the term means the spread of the message of Islam, which is how I understand it, then it was probably revealed late when people were entering the new religion in their droves and it was spreading far and fast. In this sense, it could be quite late, as the chapter becomes about the successful propagation of Islam. It looks like the chapter was revealed when the situation it describes was already in progress.

# 5

# Conclusion

There is no Qur'anic verse that describes itself as being the first or last verse or describes a chapter as being the first or last chapter. There is no report attributed to the Prophet either that describes any verse or chapter in this way. Trying to identify potential candidates for the first and last verses and chapters using their texts is a highly speculative process that can result in so many candidates.

The one approach left is to consider the reports attributed to those who were close to the Prophet, presuming there is some truth in these narratives. There is uncertainty in this case also because one cannot be totally confident that these reports are authentic and, if so, the views expressed in them reflect accurately historical facts about the Qur'an.

When studying these reports, I tried to identify all relevant facts that would make a claim more or less likely to reflect history. I will summarize here my findings.

Verse 74.1 cannot be the first revelation. The *basmala* and the first verse of the chapter of *Fātiḥa*, if the *basmala* is not considered one of its verses, are highly unlikely to have been the first revelations. The report about an unspecified verse should be dismissed.

I have concluded that, as reported on the authority of ʿĀ'isha, verse 96.1 is highly likely to be the first verse that was revealed to the Prophet. I also think that the first five verses of chapter 96 must have been revealed at the same time, as they represent one unit:

> Read in the name of your Lord who has created, (96.1) created man from a clot. (96.2) Read, and your Lord is the most generous (96.3) who has taught by the pen, (96.4) taught man that which he did not know (96.5).

This means that 96 was the first chapter to be revealed.

What about the chapter whose revelation was completed first? This is not a question that can be answered with any reasonable level of confidence.

As to the last verse of the Qur'an, nine of the ten claims have to be dismissed: 2.278, 2.278-280, 2.282, 3.195, 4.93, 4.176, 9.5, 9.128-129, and 18.110. Only this verse is a possible, though unlikely, candidate:

> Fear the day when you shall be returned to Allah, then each soul shall be paid what it has earned, and they shall not be wronged. (2.281)

The literature is highly ambiguous and confused about its use of the term "last chapter." The three candidate chapters are all late. Chapter 110 is likely to have been revealed late in Medina. Chapters 5 and 9 also both contain a number of verses that must have been revealed late. Any attempt to be more specific about the "last chapter" would be highly speculative.

# References


Abū ʿUbaid al-Qāsim b. Sallām. *Faḍā'il al-Qur'an*, edited by Marwān al-ʿAṭiyya, Muḥsin Kharāba, and Wafā' Taqī al-Dīn, Damascus: Dār Ibn Kathīr, 2000.

Aḥmad bin Ḥanbal. *Musnad al-Imām Aḥmad bin Ḥanbal*, edited by Shuʿaib al-Arna'ūṭ et al., 50 vols, Beirut: Mu'assasat al-Risāla, 1995–2001.

Al-Baihaqī, Aḥmad b. al-Ḥusain. *Al-Sunan al-Kubrā*, edited by Muḥammad ʿAṭā', 11 vols, Beirut: Dār al-Kutub al-ʿIlmiyya, 2003.

Al-Baihaqī, Aḥmad bin al-Ḥusain. *Dalā'il al-Nubuwwa*, edited by ʿAbd al-Muʿṭī Qalʿachī, 7 vols, Beirut: Dār al-Kutub al-ʿIlmiyya, 1988.

Al-Bāqillāni, Abū Bakr Ibn al-Ṭayyib. *Al-Intiṣār Lil-Qur'an*, edited by Muḥammad ʿIṣām al-Quḍāt, 2 vols, Beirut: Dār Ibn Ḥazm.

Al-Bukhārī, Muḥammad. *Al-Jāmiʿ al-Ṣaḥīḥ*, edited by ʿAbd al-Qādir al-Ḥamad, 3 vols, Riyadh: ʿAbd al-Qādir al-Ḥamad, 2008.

Fatoohi, Louay. *Abrogation in the Qur'an and Islamic Law: A Critical Study of the Concept of "Naskh" and its Impact*, New York: Routledge, 2012.

Ibn Abī Shaiba, ʿAbd Allāh. *Al-Muṣannaf li-Ibn Abī Shaiba*, edited by Usāma b. Muḥammad, 15 vols, Cairo: Al-Fārūq al-Ḥadītha lil-Ṭibāʿa wal-Nashir, 2007–2008.

Ibn ʿAqīla al-Makkī, Jamāl al-Dīn. *Al-Ziyāda wal-Iḥsān fī ʿUlūm al-Qur'an*, Shārija: Markaz al-Buḥūth Wal-Dirāsāt, 2006.

Ibn Ḥajar, Aḥmad bin ʿAlī. *Fatḥ al-Bārī bi-Sharḥ Ṣaḥīḥ al-Bukhārī*, edited by Muḥib al-Dīn al-Khaṭīb, Muḥammad F. ʿAbd al-Bāqī, and Quṣay Muḥib al-Dīn al-Khaṭīb, 13 vols, Cairo: Dār al-Rayyān lil-Turāth, 1987.

Ibn Hishām, ʿAbd al-Malik. *Sīrat al-Nabī*, edited by Fatḥī al-Dābūllī, 4 vols, Tanta: Dār al-Ṣaḥāba lil-Turāth, 1995.

Ibn Kathīr, ʿImād al-Dīn Abī al-Fīdā' Ismāʿīl. *Tafsīr al-Qur'an al-ʿAẓīm*, edited by Muṣṭafā al-Sayyid Muḥammad et al., 15 vols, Giza: Mu'assasat Qurṭuba, 2000.

Ibn Māja, Muḥammad. *Al-Sunan*, edited by Shuʿaib al-Arna'ūṭ et al, 5 vols, Damascus: Dār al-Risāla al-ʿIlmiyya, 2009.

Mḥīsin, Muḥammad. *Tārīkh al-Qur'an al-Karīm*, Jadda: Dār al-Aṣfahānī, 1393 H.

Muslim, Abū al-Ḥusain. *Ṣaḥīḥ Muslim*, edited by Muḥammad ʿAbd al-Bāqī, 5 vols, Cairo: Dār al-Ḥadīth, 1991.

Al-Nasā'ī, Aḥmad b. Shuʿaib. *Al-Mujtabā min al-*

*Sunan*, edited by Bait al-Afkār al-Duwaliyya, Riyadh: International Ideas Home, 1999.

Al-Nasā'ī, Aḥmad b. Shuʿaib. *Al-Sunan al-Kubrā*, edited by Ḥasan Shalabī, 12 vols, Beirut: Mu'ssasat al-Risāla, 2001.

Al-Qaṭṭān, Mannāʿ. *Mabāḥith fī ʿUlūm al-Qur'an*, Cairo: Maktabat Wahba, 1995.

Al-Suyūṭī, Jalāl al-Dīn. *Al-Itqān fī ʿUlūm al-Qur'an*, edited by Markaz al-Dirāsāt al-Islāmiyya, 7 vols, Medina: Mujammaʿ al-Malik Fahad li-Ṭibāʿat al-Muṣḥaf al-Sharīf, 2005.

Al-Ṭabarī, Muḥammad bin Jarīr. *Jāmiʿ al-Bayān ʿan Ta'wīl 'Āy al-Qur'an*, edited by ʿAbd Allāh al-Turkī, 24 vols, Al-Ihsa: Dār Hajr, 2001.

Al-Ṭabarī, Muḥammad bin Jarīr. *Tarīkh al-Umam wal-Mulūk*, edited by Abū Ṣuhaib al-Karmī, Jordan: Bait al-Afkār al-Duwalyya, undated.

Al-Ṭabaṭabā'ī, Muḥammad. *Al-Mīzān fī Tafsīr al-Qur'an*, 22 vols, Beirut: Mu'assasat al-Aʿlamī lil-Maṭbūʿāt, 1997.

Ṭāhā, ʿĀbidīn Ṭāhā. "Tartīb Suwar al-Qur'an: Dirāsa Taḥlīliyya li-Aqwāl al-ʿUlamā'." *Majallat al-Buḥūth wal-Dirāsāt al-Qur'āniyya*, vol 5-6, no. 9 (21-94), undated.

Al-Tirmidhī, Muḥammad. *Al-Jāmiʿ al-Kabīr*, edited

by Bashshār Maʿrūf, 6 vols, Beirut: Dār al-Gharb al-Islāmī, 1996.

Al-Wāḥidī, Abū al-Ḥasan. *Asbāb al-Nuzūl*, edited by Kāmāl Basyūnī Zaghlūl, Beirut: Dār al-Kutub al-ʿIlmiyya, 1991.

Al-Zamakhsharī, Jār Allah. *Al-Kashshāf*, edited by ʿĀdil ʿAbd al-Mawjūd and ʿAlī Muʿawwaḍ, 6 vols, Riyadh: Maktabat al-ʿBīkān, 1998.

Al-Zarkashī, Badr al-Dīn. *Al-Burhān fī ʿUlūm al-Qur'an*, edited by Muḥammad Ibrāhīm, 4 vols, Cairo: Maktabat Dār al-Turāth, 1984.

Al-Zarqānī, Muḥammad. *Manāhil al-ʿIrfān fī ʿUlūm al-Qur'an*, edited by Fawwāz Zamarlī, 2 vols, Beirut: Dār al-Kitāb al-ʿArabī, 1995.

# Notes

[1] Zarqānī, *Manāhil al-ʿIrfān fī ʿUlūm al-Qur'an*, I, p. 202.

[2] Ibid., part 1, pp. 287-293.

[3] Ṭāhā, *Tartīb Suwar al-Qur'an*.

[4] Aḥmad, *Musnad al-Imām Aḥmad bin Ḥanbal*, XXIX, no. 17918, p. 441.

[5] Bāqillāni, *al-Intiṣār lil-Qur'an*, I, pp. 238, 245.

[6] In order to place any important figure and scholar in his historical context, I have mentioned his Hjiri year of death when his name is first mentioned.

[7] The Prophet's reply may also be understood as "I will not read."

[8] Bukhārī, *al-Jāmiʿ al-Ṣaḥīḥ*, I, no. 3, pp. 49-50.

[9] Aḥmad, *Musnad al-Imām Aḥmad bin Ḥanbal*, XLIII, no. 25959, pp. 112-114.

[10] Muslim, *Ṣaḥīḥ Muslim*, I, no. 252, pp. 139-142.

[11] Ṭabarī, *Jāmiʿ al-Bayān ʿan Ta'wīl Āy al-Qur'an*, XXIV, p. 530.

[12] Abū ʿUbaid, *Faḍā'il al-Qur'an*, p. 364.

[13] Ṭabarī, *Jāmiʿ al-Bayān ʿan Ta'wīl Āy al-Qur'an*, XXIV, p. 529.

[14] Ṭabarī, *Tarīkh al-Umam wal-Mulūk*, p. 309.

[15] Ibn Abī Shaiba, *Al-Muṣannaf li-Ibn Abī Shaiba*, X, no. 30825, 30827, 30828, p. 63.

[16] Ibn Kathīr, *Tafsīr al-Qur'an al-ʿAẓīm*, XIV, p. 175.

[17] Suyūṭī, *Al-Itqān fī ʿUlūm al-Qur'an*, I, p. 166.

[18] Ṭabaṭabā'ī, *Al-Mīzān fī Tafsīr al-Qur'an*, XX, p. 370.
[19] Zarqānī, *Manāhil al-'Irfān fī 'Ulūm al-Qur'an*, I, p. 77.
[20] Qaṭṭān, *Mabāḥith fī 'Ulūm al-Qur'an*, p. 61.
[21] Ṭabarī, *Jāmi' al-Bayān 'an Ta'wīl Āy al-Qur'an*, XXIII, p. 534.
[22] Ibid., XXIII, p. 400.
[23] Muslim, *Ṣaḥīḥ Muslim*, I, no. 257, p. 144.
[24] Bukhārī, *al-Jāmi' al-Ṣaḥīḥ*, III, no. 4734, pp. 149-150.
[25] Ibid., III, no. 4736, p. 150.
[26] Ibid., III, no. 4765, pp. 161-162.
[27] Abū 'Ubaid, *Faḍā'il al-Qur'an*, p. 363.
[28] Muslim, *Ṣaḥīḥ Muslim*, I, no. 252, p. 143.
[29] Ṭabarī, *Jāmi' al-Bayān 'an Ta'wīl Āy al-Qur'an*, XXIII, p. 400-401.
[30] Wāḥidī, Asbāb al-Nuzūl, p. 15.
[31] Ibn 'Aqīla al-Makkī, *Al-Ziyāda wal-Iḥsān fī 'Ulūm al-Qur'an*, p. 175.
[32] Suyūṭī, *Al-Itqān fī 'Ulūm al-Qur'an*, I, pp. 162-163.
[33] Ṭabarī, *Jāmi' al-Bayān 'an Ta'wīl Āy al-Qur'an*, XXIV, pp. 528-529.
[34] Abū 'Ubaid, *Faḍā'il al-Qur'an*, p. 364.
[35] Ṭabarī, *Jāmi' al-Bayān 'an Ta'wīl Āy al-Qur'an*, XXIV, pp. 529-530.
[36] Ibid., XXIV, pp. 485-486.
[37] Baihaqī, *Dalā'il al-Nubuwwa*, II, p. 158.
[38] Bāqillāni, *al-Intiṣār lil-Qur'an*, I, p. 241; Wāḥidī, *Asbāb al-Nuzūl*, p. 22.

[39] Baihaqī, *Al-Sunan al-Kubrā*, II, no. 2385, 2387, p. 66.
[40] Muslim, *Ṣaḥīḥ Muslim*, I, no. 399, p. 299.
[41] Baihaqī, *Dalā'il al-Nubuwwa*, II, p. 159.
[42] Abū 'Ubaid, *Faḍā'il al-Qur'an*, p. 367.
[43] Zamakhsharī, *Al-Kashshāf*, VI, p. 403.
[44] Zarkashī, *Al-Burhān fī 'Ulūm al-Qur'an*, I, pp. 207-208.
[45] See, for example, Ibn 'Aqīla al-Makkī, *Al-Ziyāda wal-Iḥsān fī 'Ulūm al-Qur'an*, pp. 176-177; Suyūṭī, *Al-Itqān fī 'Ulūm al-Qur'an*, I, pp. 163-165; Zarqānī, *Manāhil al-'Irfān fī 'Ulūm al-Qur'an*, I, pp. 79-80; Qaṭṭān, *Mabāḥith fī 'Ulūm al-Qur'an*, p. 63.
[46] Ṭabarī, *Jāmi' al-Bayān 'an Ta'wīl Āy al-Qur'an*, I, p. 111.
[47] Wāḥidī, *Asbāb al-Nuzūl*, p. 14.
[48] Ibid., p. 20.
[49] Suyūṭī, *Al-Itqān fī 'Ulūm al-Qur'an*, I, p. 165.
[50] Zarqānī, *Manāhil al-'Irfān fī 'Ulūm al-Qur'an*, I, p. 80.
[51] Ibn Kathīr, *Tafsīr al-Qur'an al-'Aẓīm*, I, p. 174.
[52] Abū 'Ubaid, *Faḍā'il al-Qur'an*, p. 365.
[53] Suyūṭī, *Al-Itqān fī 'Ulūm al-Qur'an*, I, p. 166.
[54] Bukhārī, *al-Jāmi' al-Ṣaḥīḥ*, III, no. 4803, p. 173.
[55] Zarkashī, *Al-Burhān fī 'Ulūm al-Qur'an*, I, pp. 199-202.
[56] Ibid., I, p. 200.
[57] Bukhārī, *al-Jāmi' al-Ṣaḥīḥ*, III, no. 4361, p. 22.
[58] Suyūṭī, *Al-Itqān fī 'Ulūm al-Qur'an*, I, p. 176.
[59] Aḥmad, *Musnad al-Imām Aḥmad bin Ḥanbal*, I, no. 246, p. 361.
[60] Ṭabarī, *Jāmi' al-Bayān 'an Ta'wīl Āy al-Qur'an*, V, p. 66.

[61] Nasā'ī, *Al-Sunan al-Kubrā*, X, no. 10991, p. 40.
[62] Ṭabaṭabā'ī, *Al-Mīzān fī Tafsīr al-Qur'an*, II, p. 431.
[63] Ṭabarī, *Jāmi' al-Bayān 'an Ta'wīl Āy al-Qur'an*, V, p. 68.
[64] Abū 'Ubaid, *Faḍā'il al-Qur'an*, p. 370.
[65] Zamakhsharī, *Al-Kashshāf*, I, p. 510.
[66] Ibn Kathīr, *Tafsīr al-Qur'an al-'Aẓīm*, II, p. 503.
[67] Baihaqī, *Dalā'il al-Nubuwwa*, VII, p. 137.
[68] Zamakhsharī, *Al-Kashshāf*, I, p. 510.
[69] Bukhārī, *al-Jāmi' al-Ṣaḥīḥ*, I, no. 2033, p. 545.
[70] Ibn Ḥajar, Fatḥ al-Bārī bi-Sharḥ Ṣaḥīḥ al-Bukhārī, VIII, no. 4544, p. 53.
[71] Zarqānī, *Manāhil al-'Irfān fī 'Ulūm al-Qur'an*, I, pp. 81-82.
[72] Abū 'Ubaid, *Faḍā'il al-Qur'an*, p. 369.
[73] Suyūṭī, *Al-Itqān fī 'Ulūm al-Qur'an*, I, p. 180.
[74] Ibid., I, p. 180.
[75] Ibn Kathīr, *Tafsīr al-Qur'an al-'Aẓīm*, III, p. 306.
[76] Suyūṭī, *Al-Itqān fī 'Ulūm al-Qur'an*, I, pp. 185-186.
[77] Ṭabarī, *Jāmi' al-Bayān 'an Ta'wīl Āy al-Qur'an*, VI, p. 320.
[78] Bukhārī, *al-Jāmi' al-Ṣaḥīḥ*, III, no. 4405, p. 37.
[79] Nasā'ī, *Al-Mujtabā min al-Sunan*, no. 4000, p. 421.
[80] Bukhārī, *al-Jāmi' al-Ṣaḥīḥ*, III, no. 4420, p. 40.
[81] Suyūṭī, *Al-Itqān fī 'Ulūm al-Qur'an*, I, p. 180.
[82] Ibn Māja, *Al-Sunan*, I, no. 70, p. 49.
[83] Fatoohi, *Abrogation in the Qur'an and Islamic Law*, pp. 114-121.

[84] Ṭabarī, *Jāmiʿ al-Bayān ʿan Ta'wīl Āy al-Qur'an*, XII, p. 102.
[85] Bukhārī, *al-Jāmiʿ al-Ṣaḥīḥ*, III, no. 4494, p. 61.
[86] Ṭabarī, *Jāmiʿ al-Bayān ʿan Ta'wīl Āy al-Qur'an*, XV, pp. 441-442.
[87] Tirmidhī, *Al-Jāmiʿ al-Kabīr*, V, no. 3063, p. 150.
[88] Baihaqī, *Al-Sunan al-Kubrā*, VII, no. 13979, pp. 278-279.
[89] Nasā'ī, *Al-Sunan al-Kubrā*, X, no. 11073, p. 79.
[90] Baihaqī, *Al-Sunan al-Kubrā*, VII, no. 13978, p. 278.
[91] Bukhārī, *al-Jāmiʿ al-Ṣaḥīḥ*, I, no. 45, p. 63.
[92] Ṭabarī, *Jāmiʿ al-Bayān ʿan Ta'wīl Āy al-Qur'an*, VIII, p. 80.
[93] Bukhārī, *al-Jāmiʿ al-Ṣaḥīḥ*, III, no. 4469, p. 54.
[94] Nasā'ī, *Al-Sunan al-Kubrā*, X, no. 11148, p. 111.
[95] Ibn Abī Shaiba, *Al-Muṣannaf li-Ibn Abī Shaiba*, X, no. 30821, p. 62.
[96] Bukhārī, *al-Jāmiʿ al-Ṣaḥīḥ*, II, no. 4195, p. 500.
[97] Muslim, *Ṣaḥīḥ Muslim*, III, no. 1618, p. 1237.
[98] Ibn Hishām, *Sīrat al-Nabī*, IV, p. 220.
[99] Tirmidhī, *Al-Jāmiʿ al-Kabīr*, V, no. 3086, p. 166.
[100] Nasā'ī, *Al-Sunan al-Kubrā*, X, no. 11649, p. 349.
[101] Muslim, *Ṣaḥīḥ Muslim*, IV, no. 3024, p. 2318.
[102] Ibn Abī Shaiba, *Al-Muṣannaf li-Ibn Abī Shaiba*, XII, no. 36895, p. 317.
[103] Bukhārī, *al-Jāmiʿ al-Ṣaḥīḥ*, II, no. 4132, p. 484.
[104] Ibid., III, no. 4780, p. 166.

www.ingramcontent.com/pod-product-compliance
Lightning Source LLC
Chambersburg PA
CBHW020557030426
42337CB00013B/1127
* 9 7 8 1 9 0 6 3 4 2 1 8 0 *